CHINESE
MIGRATIONS

Judith Kendra

Wayland

Titles in the Migrations series

African Migrations
Chinese Migrations
Indian Migrations
Jewish Migrations

Acknowledgement:
With many thanks to Jill Anderson

First published in 1994 by Wayland (Publishers) Ltd
61 Western Road, Hove, East Sussex, BN3 1JD, England

© Copyright 1994 Wayland (Publishers) Ltd

Series editor: Cath Senker
Editor: Margot Richardson
Series design: Suzie Hooper
Book design: Pardoe Blacker Ltd
Cover design: Simon Borrough

British Library Cataloguing in Publication Data
Kendra, Judith
Chinese Migrations (Migrations series)
I. Title   II. Series
304.80951

ISBN 0-7502-1229-2

Printed and bound in Italy by G. Canale & C.S.p.A., Turin

Links with the National Curriculum

HISTORY

KS 2 Core Unit 4: Britain since 1930 (immigration and emigration; popular culture).

KS3 Core Unit 3: Expansion, Trade and Industry – Britain 1750 to 1900. Especially chapter 2 which looks at the concepts of empire and trading.
    Core Unit 4: The Twentieth-Century World.

KS 3 Supplementary Unit B: a unit involving the study of a past non-European socirty, for example, Imperial China from the first Emperor to Kubla Khan.

GEOGRAPHY*

 AT 4 Human Geography

Level 3 particularly, and also levels 5 and 7.

The cross-curricular theme of Citizenship, particuarly component 2: A Pluralist Society, and also component 3: Being a Citizen.

* as of May 1994

CONTENTS

Main Chinese Migrations

CANADA

BRITISH COLUMBIA

NORTH

Vancouver

AMERICA

Toronto

Sacramento

USA

New York

San Francisco

Washington DC

San Diego ● Phoenix

ATLANTIC OCEAN

CENTRAL

AMERICA

WEST INDIES

PACIFIC OCEAN

KEY

Areas of the world to which many Chinese people have migrated.

EUROPE

London

Paris
FRANCE

AFRICA

CHINA

Beijing

SICHUAN
PROVINCE

Yangzte river

JAPAN

Yokohama

TAIWAN

Hong Kong

PACIFIC OCEAN

MYANMAR
(BURMA)

Rangoon

THAILAND

Bangkok

CAMBODIA

VIETNAM

Pattani

MALAYSIA

Singapore

SUMATRA

SOUTH EAST
ASIA

PHILIPPINES

INDONESIA

AUSTRALIA

Sydney

NEW
ZEALAND

SOUTH EAST CHINA

FUJIAN
PROVINCE

Guilin

GUANGDONG
PROVINCE

Canton
(Guangzhou)

Swatow

Hong Kong

SOUTH CHINA SEA

5

1 A new life

'My name is Meili Yip, though people here call me Mary. I'm ten years old and live in London with my parents. They came to Britain in 1984 from Hong Kong. My grandparents on my mother's side live in Canton [China] and those on my father's side live in Hong Kong. One of my uncles lives with his family in Vancouver [Canada] and another one lives in San Francisco [USA]. My sister is married and lives in Hong Kong.'

This example shows you how migration from one country to another can affect a family, especially a Chinese one. But why do people migrate in the first place?

People migrate for a number of different reasons. Some leave their country for what they think are better opportunities elsewhere. Being tempted away like this is called a 'pull' factor. Other people migrate because they are forced to do so. Reasons for these 'push' factors can be such things as war, famine, floods, unemployment or prejudice in the country they are leaving behind.

A Chinese migrant becomes an Australian citizen. In recent years, Australia has welcomed people from many South East Asian countries, including China.

What must it be like to leave your own country, possibly for ever? Those who want to migrate will be looking forward to seeing new places, trying different food and finding different jobs. Some will be hoping to make their fortunes. They might dream of returning home one day wearing expensive clothes and bringing gifts for their relatives – just to show how successful they have become. Yet not all migrants will do well abroad. Some will barely make a living.

For those who do not want to migrate, the picture is a very different one. If they are being forced to leave because of war or discrimination, they may have to leave everything they possess behind. They may have a terrible sea journey or a very difficult, long walk to make before they reach another country where they are safe.

San Francisco's Chinatown. When the Chinese move abroad they try to support each other, and recreate Chinese culture in their new countries.

In a new country, the first migrants try hard to keep up their language, religion and the way of life they used to have in the old country. They try to make sure their children learn about the culture they have come from, as well as the new one they are now a part of. This becomes harder as more and more generations are born away from 'home'.

Most migrants, of course, will miss the friends and families they left behind. They will do their best to keep in contact, if this is possible. Some will hope to return to their homeland when they are older, if they are allowed to return and can afford to do so.

Chinese migration

Chinese people have a long and interesting history of migration. Tens of millions have left China over the centuries, and have remained settled abroad. Most of them emigrated in the nineteenth and twentieth centuries, and most of them, in recent years, have gone to English-speaking parts of the globe.

A view from Moonhill, near Guilin in southern China. Even if Chinese migrants live thousands of kilometres away in another country, they still feel attached to China.

Most Chinese migrants came from two provinces on the southern coast of China: Guangdong and Fujian (also called Kwangtung and Fukien). Fujian is about the same size as England, or the state of Ohio, and is mostly covered by mountains. Guangdong is larger and contains the important city of Guangzhou (also known as Canton), with Hong Kong not far away.

People speak a large number of different languages and dialects in the south of China (whereas most people in the north of China speak just one language, Mandarin). Those living in Fujian mostly speak Hokkien. Those living near Swatow in Guangdong speak Teochiu (also called Chaozhou or Chiuchow). Some in both provinces belong to the Hakka speech group.

Not surprisingly, those emigrating prefer to go to a place where the Chinese already living there speak the same dialect as they do. This is why, in the past, Hokkiens tended to sail to the Philippines, Singapore, Malaya (Malaysia), Indonesia, Burma (Myanmar) and southern Siam (Thailand). In contrast, Teochius often went to Bangkok (the capital of Thailand) and the Cantonese to the USA.

In Guangdong and Fujian provinces, a village is usually made up of just one big family, including aunts, uncles and cousins, so they all have the same surname. They are proud to be able to trace back their family trees for generations. The importance they give to their family ties means that when they emigrate they try to live close to each other and to help each other as much as possible. This pattern has been clearly seen in some cities in the USA. For example, for many years, most of the Chinese in Sacramento had the surname of Fong, most of those in San Diego were called Hom and most of those in Phoenix were called Tang.

Family links, especially between generations, are very important to the Chinese.

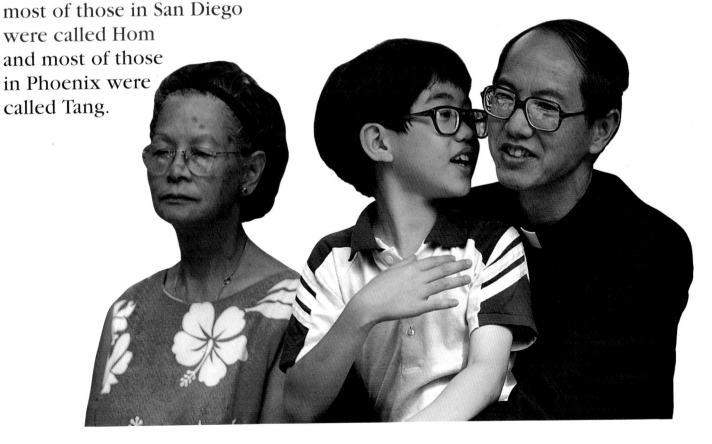

No matter where he or she is living, a Chinese person has very strong feelings about the place his or her ancestors come from and are buried in. Traditionally, the eldest son was expected to look after his parents during their lifetimes. He was also expected to say special prayers in front of their graves (and the graves of their ancestors). Each family had a grave of its own, and if someone died away from home his or her body would be brought back to be buried

A shrine to ancestors in a Chinese temple. The plaques give their names, and the photographs show their likenesses.

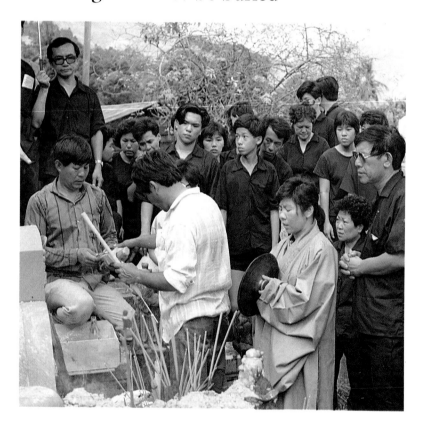

Mourners at a Chinese funeral in Malaysia. Performing the correct rituals at death is extremely important.

there, if that was at all possible. These days, although these ideals about 'home' remain, they are not often put into practice.

A well-known poem by Li Po shows the attachment of Chinese people to their home:

> *So bright a gleam at the foot of my bed –*
> *Could there have been a frost already?*
> *Lifting myself to look, I see that it is moonlight.*
> *Lowering my head, I dream that I am home.*

2 Pirates and traders

China is a nation with a rich and glorious past. This vast country has been the centre of an incredible civilization which has been in continuous existence since at least 2000 BC. The Chinese invented the arts of printing and tea-making, as well as the manufacture of paper, porcelain and silk. These things, among many, many others, were so in advance of their time that they seemed almost magical to outsiders. It was centuries before people in other countries were able to make silk or porcelain themselves, for example. It was not surprising, therefore, that foreigners wanted to trade with China. However the Chinese, though very proud of their achievements, did not always want to trade with them.

The Chinese people called their emperor The Son of Heaven because he was thought to be in a middle place, between heaven and people. They believed he was the most important ruler of 'all under heaven', or the whole world. Therefore, they divided the earth's peoples into Chinese and 'Barbarians', or those living in other countries who were not yet lucky enough to be ruled by The Son of Heaven.

A painting of the eighteenth-century Chinese emperor Kein-Lung.

Barbarians were allowed to come to the imperial court to ask for special trading or political favours, so long as they brought presents (or tribute) for the emperors. Ordinary Chinese people, however, were not fully allowed to trade with foreigners until 1683, and going abroad was frowned on by The Sons of Heaven

Europeans approaching important Chinese people. Barbarians were expected to kneel in front of the emperor.

until the end of the nineteenth century. There were many laws to stop them doing so, like this one in 1799:

All officers of government, soldiers, and private citizens, who clandestinely [secretly] proceed to sea to trade, or who [go] to foreign islands for the purpose of inhabiting and cultivating the same, shall . . . suffer death by being beheaded.

However, there were still many people who disobeyed the emperors by sailing away in their junks (Chinese ships) to South East Asia to try to make their fortunes. Throughout the fifteenth and sixteenth centuries, for example, these seamen called at the ports of such countries now known as Thailand, Malaysia, Taiwan, the Philippines, Indonesia and Vietnam. Some of these traders settled in the foreign countries they visited and others became pirates.

A CHINESE PIRATE

Lin Tao-ch'ien was one of the most wanted outlaws of the South China Seas in the sixteenth century. He, together with a band of 2,000 men, escaped from Fujian province and sailed to Siam (now called Thailand). These men formed the centre of a Chinese settlement at the port of Pattani. Here, they schemed and plotted how to raid not only the coasts of South East Asia, but also that of China itself. Eventually, Lin married the daughter of a local chieftain and ruled over a part of Malaya (now Malaysia) himself. [1]

From the sixteenth to the nineteenth centuries the Dutch, Portuguese, French and British were looking for trading opportunities outside their own countries. They took control of different parts of the world, including parts of Asia, and called these places their empires. As these empires expanded there were possibilities for many people to make some money within them. These possibilities were 'pull' factors for adventurous Chinese people. Wherever tin was being mined, tobacco or sugar being planted, rubber being tapped, or pepper being cultivated, you could be sure that some Chinese would also be there making a living.

Chinese pirate junks (the large boats) being attacked in the Opium War, 1849.

During the nineteenth century, the British began selling large quantities of the drug called opium to people in China. People became addicted to it very easily, which meant that they spent large amounts of money on it, damaged their health, and were not always able to work. This brought hardship to many people.

An opium den – where people came to take the drug – in Shanghai, 1910.

The opium trade, although it was against the law, made much money for the British and paid for the legal trade they hoped to expand in the country. In 1840, to enforce their position, the British started a war with China, later called the First Opium War.

China lost the war, and so agreed to allow the British to occupy the island of Hong Kong, and to allow foreigners to trade in five of the ports along its southern coast. Gradually the French and the Americans were given the same rights to trade with China.

The opening of the ports brought many foreign ships to China and far more possibilities of trade than ever before. This, in turn, caused many Chinese to move from their inland villages to the coast in search of work. From there, thousands and thousands sailed all over the world, migrating for better opportunities and a more stable place to live.

As well as South East Asia, Chinese people travelled to Africa, North, Central and South America, the Caribbean, Britain, and many other places far away from their homeland. They lived not just in the coastal regions and the capital cities but also deep in the heart of their new countries.

They first went to Britain, for example, in the ships owned by the East India Company, which traded in Asia. Mostly seamen, they settled in London, Liverpool, Cardiff, Bristol and Glasgow. In 1851, there were only 78 of them in the country. Twenty years later, there were 202. By 1881 this number had increased to 665 (mostly because several shipping companies in Liverpool had started trading with China). By 1911, there were 1,319. Generally, they earned their livings by running laundries, shops, restaurants, and lodging houses which looked after Chinese sailors.

Chinese migrants on a ship taking them to the USA, 1884. The first migrants were always men: women joined them only when they were settled in the new country.

AW BOON HAW: THE TIGER BALM KING

Named after the tiger (*haw*), Aw Boon Haw was born in 1882 in Burma (now Myanmar) to which his father had migrated from Fujian province in southern China. Aw Boon Haw and his brother inherited their father's herbalist shop, and in 1926 they moved to Singapore.

Here, Aw Boon Haw began to make and sell a strong-smelling ointment. It was called Tiger Balm and was supposed to be able to cure almost any ailment. The recipe was a secret but many people believed that it contained parts of a ground-up tiger. It has sold extremely well for years throughout South East Asia, making a fortune for Aw Boon Haw. It can also be bought in some Western countries today.

Aw Boon Haw used the sign of the tiger on many things. For example, the car he owned looked like a tiger. Its headlamps were the eyes and the horn roared like a wild beast. The body was painted in black, orange and white stripes. Everyone knew when its owner was on the move.

Tiger Balm can still be bought in many countries today.

With his fabulous fortune, Aw Boon Haw also made the Tiger Balm Gardens in Singapore. These were a little like an early kind of Disneyland with very brightly-coloured statues telling vivid stories of murders, myths and legends. There were figures bleeding pints of painted blood, concrete kangaroos, women with chickens' heads and other extraordinary things to see. [2]

3 Hard labour

During the nineteenth century, many Chinese left their homeland because they were forced to do so. One of those 'push' factors was a population explosion in China. Because there were too many people it became very difficult for some to find enough to eat, to get work and to look after their families. Many therefore left to seek their fortunes elsewhere.

Another 'push' factor was the Taiping Rebellion which took place between 1850 and 1864. This uprising, against the authority of the emperor, caused tremendous damage inside China: more than 600 cities were destroyed and many thousands of people moved southwards and then fled abroad to escape the fighting.

Beggars in Beijing, in about 1860. Poverty encouraged many people to try their luck in other countries.

Two methods of emigration became especially well known. One was the credit-ticket system, also known as free emigration. This was a way of receiving a free passage on board ship. If you could not afford the fare you were given a piece of paper or a 'ticket'. This showed your name, age, the place you had come from and the place you were going to. When you arrived at your destination, the cost of your sea voyage was paid by a friend, relative or your new employer until you could afford to pay them back. Chinese people who journeyed to Australia, Thailand, Singapore, Malaya and North America often went under this system.

Another form of emigration was the coolie or indentured-labour system. Coolie is believed to come from the Chinese word *ku-li*, meaning hard strength, and was applied to the thousands of men who were given a 'contract'. This meant they had agreed to work for someone abroad for a fixed number of years. Contract labourers were sent out from China to places throughout the world from 1845 onwards.

Sometimes, a man might have been down on his luck. He might, for instance, have owed money, been a prisoner, or been starving. It was just this sort of person who could have been easily persuaded, or even tricked, into becoming a coolie. Once he had signed the contract and arrived in his new country he became virtually the slave of his new master, just as Africans had been slaves before him. In fact, Chinese coolies often took the place of African slaves as cheap workers in the different European empires. And sometimes they were treated just as badly.

Chinese labourers were often treated like slaves by their new masters. Their work was hard, and it was many years until they were free again.

Coolies had to endure appalling conditions on the ships that took them to their new countries. These ships were almost always extremely overcrowded and their human cargo was often kept chained up in case of rebellion, or mutiny. A ship that was meant to carry, say, 300 men might have 600 in its hold. The journeys were so terrible that, in the 1850s, as many as 15 to 45 per cent of coolies died on their way to the Western hemisphere.

Golden opportunities

Stories of making a fortune from discovering gold were common in the middle of the nineteenth century. Chinese migrants, along with other hopeful people from all over the world, rushed to look for it in California, British Columbia, Australia and New Zealand in particular.

Chinese miners panning for gold in the California gold fields, mid-nineteenth century.

Thousands of gold prospectors poured to the USA's west coast. In 1852 alone, for example, 20,000 Chinese passed through San Francisco on their way to the gold fields. For a time, there was so much work to be done in California and so few people to do it that prices were very high. Apparently some miners found it cheaper to send their dirty washing all the way back to Hong Kong to be laundered than to have it cleaned locally!

Thousands of credit-ticket emigrants left the area of the Pearl River Delta in southern China to look for gold in Australia. As many as 11,500 went to Victoria in 1855, and 12,500 to New South Wales in 1858. Sometimes, though, the local people did not like having so many newcomers arriving in their neighbourhood.

Chinese workers were often thrown out of Australian gold-mining camps by other miners.

When the US railways were finished, many Chinese labourers stayed, and turned to other work.

Fights, some of them racist ones, broke out. For example, in 1861, a thousand white miners in Lambing Flat in Australia went to attack the Chinese migrants among them. They marched behind a band, shouting as they went:

> *Rule Britannia! Britannia rules the waves!*
> *No more Chinamen shall land in New South Wales!*

Back in the USA, when gold began to run out, the Chinese became involved in making the new railways. It took most of the 1860s to lay a track right across the continent, through mountains and desert, and the Chinese provided much of the labour to build it. It was such hard work that many Chinese lost their lives in the attempt. The same thing happened in Canada. In 1870, for example, a newspaper reported that the bones of 1,200 railway workers (weighing 9,000 kg) were shipped back to China for burial. (As we have seen, the Chinese prefer their bodies to be buried at 'home' if this is at all possible.)

Wartime

Not many people know that the Chinese also took part in the First World War, on the side of the Western Allies. At first they were employed in Europe by the British and French. They helped in the factories, on the railways, in the dockyards and in other places. This meant that the French and British were free to go to the front line and fight.

When China entered the war in August 1917, however, the Chinese became involved on the battlefields themselves. They buried casualties, dug trenches and took on other duties. As a result, many were killed and some were buried on the French coast. The largest cemetery for Chinese is at Noyelles-sur-Mer in north-west France and contains 838 graves.

During the Second World War, many US and Canadian Chinese served in the armies of these two countries in the fight against Japan.

4 Needed, wanted or hated?

For centuries, the Chinese living abroad have sent money home. They have done this mostly to help their families still living in China, but also for business reasons. Over the years, these remittances have helped many people inside China. They have also helped the country as a whole. Between 1929 and 1941, for example, Chinese people living overseas sent back as much as US $80–100 million every year.

A decorative arch, built by Chinese community in Singapore, to celebrate a British royal visit in 1922.

During various times in its history, the Chinese government made a special effort to look after Chinese people living abroad. This was partly to keep them loyal to China and partly so that their remittances would continue to arrive. From about 1920, therefore, schoolteachers were sent out from China to teach children of the Chinese communities in South East Asia. The children learned about Chinese culture and also how to speak the Mandarin language. In this way, they continued to feel close to China. Yet this sometimes made them unpopular in their adopted countries because they seemed to care more for their old country than for their new one.

Fighting the Japanese in the streets of Shanghai, 1932. Although they lived thousands of kilometres away, many Chinese sent money to help the Chinese government defeat the Japanese.

When the Japanese army invaded China in 1937, the Chinese living abroad sent large sums of money to help the Chinese government. Later, when the Japanese invaded the countries of South East Asia, it was the Chinese living in them who often fought back the hardest. This was especially true in Malaya where, in the 1930s, about 40 per cent of the population was Chinese.

After the Japanese were defeated in Malaya, there was another period of fighting called the Malayan Emergency. During this new struggle in the 1950s, the Chinese were involved in fighting the British (who were ruling Malaya at the time). Eventually the British won and, between 1950 and 1952, they sent nearly 10,000 Chinese people back to China.

China accepted these refugees. However, from the 1950s onwards, it generally encouraged the Chinese people abroad to think of themselves as part of their adopted countries rather than as Chinese nationals who happened to be living in different countries.

CLOTHING IN CHINA

The illustration below was made by Stanley L. Wood (1866-1928) for a book called *Peoples of the World* in 1896. It shows how people in the West thought Chinese people looked and dressed at the time.

China is well known for its silk, which was worn by men and women of high social standing. Often, patterns were embroidered on the front and back of their ankle-length coats. The patterns would show immediately the wearer's social status. Civil servants wore bird designs, and soldiers

and sailors wore wild animal designs. Princes and ministers wore oval patterns. Their wives wore designs similar to those of their husbands.

Ordinary citizens wore long trousers that flared at the bottom and a short robe or jacket. These were usually made of cotton; silk and other fine fabrics were only worn by wealthy people.

The colour of clothing was also significant. Blue was the cheapest dye, so it was usually worn by the poor. Yellow could be worn only by the upper classes.

Red was a symbol of luck and happiness, so it was worn by brides.

After the Communist revolution in 1949, people throughout China wore a uniform of plain working clothes. Traditional silk clothing was considered a luxury.

Indonesian youths breaking into the Chinese embassy in Indonesia's capital, Jakarta, in 1967. They attacked Chinese diplomats, burned papers, and wrecked the buildings.

During the 1950s, '60s and '70s the Chinese had mixed fortunes in South East Asia. In some countries, they seemed to be needed and wanted. This was because they were often very good at business or were prepared to do jobs which other people did not want to do. In other countries, though, they were hated. One reason was because they seemed to be loyal to the Communist government in China, and this government was often unpopular abroad. Another reason was because they seemed to be making much more money than other people in the country they had joined, and were sending some of it out of the country. Sometimes the Chinese were hated for no other reason than because they were Chinese.

A temple in Cambodia where the Khmer Rouge killed many people. It is now a museum.

During the years after the Second World War, there was hardly a country in South East Asia where there was not discrimination against the Chinese. This brought a great deal of hardship to the Chinese communities in the area. For example, when the Khmer Rouge Communists took control of the capital of Cambodia in 1975, an estimated 200,000 ethnic Chinese died from starvation, disease and executions. The Khmer Rouge specifically targeted the Chinese because they believed them to be rich. As a result, about half the Chinese population in the country died.

Another country which has a bad record of violence against the Chinese is Indonesia. It has been said that in no other place have more Chinese been killed or wounded, run away or been chased away, and been more insecure than in Indonesia. Hundreds of Chinese, for example, were killed in 1966 in Sumatra (one of the islands of Indonesia). Their houses and shops were looted and slogans like this were written on the walls:

Drive out the Chinese now. You will be beheaded if you don't leave.

In other countries, such as Malaya, the Chinese faced economic discrimination. When the British left the country in 1957, the Malays held political power and the Chinese held economic power (even though they made up only one-third of the population). In order to break the influence of the Chinese, the government gave the Malays special access to education, jobs and other parts of the economic life of the country. It was not long, therefore, before small and medium-sized Chinese businesses were (and still are) having a difficult time.

1967: an injured man is helped by soldiers, after being hurt during anti-Chinese riots in Jakarta.

Vietnamese boat people sailing into Hong Kong harbour after a hard journey. The government placed them in over-crowded camps where many had to stay for several years.

In Vietnam, between 1975 and 1979, an estimated 430,000 to 466,000 ethnic Chinese fled from the country. This was as a direct result of government policies that discriminated against them. Most could take none of their belongings with them and they had no choice but to set out to sea in tiny boats, trying to escape. They tried to reach China, Hong Kong and other places in South East Asia but thousands never survived the terrible journey. This was because other countries in the area (such as Thailand and Malaysia) did not want to receive the refugees. If they caught them arriving on a beach they would tow them straight back out to sea again, to face another ordeal by storm, starvation – and also pirate fishermen. The fishermen could be especially ruthless towards them:

The refugees are robbed, raped or rescued, or all three . . . Most of them have some money, an old ten-dollar bill in a shoe or a trouser cuff . . . However, some of them have no money and that's what the fishermen can't believe. Sometimes the refugees come in [to the shore] naked. [3]

A REFUGEE'S STORY

Mr Ngoc, now in his seventies and living in London, had to escape from Vietnam by boat. 'In China, I was a teacher of Chinese literature, but I escaped because of the Japanese invasion [in 1937]. I was only twenty-three. . . I went to Hanoi [North Vietnam] and became a journalist. I worked as an editor for twenty years . . . Under the Communist regime in Vietnam, I lost my freedom of speech and lived in extreme poverty. We all wanted to leave but there was no way through the usual channels. We knew it would be very dangerous to go by boat into those strong seas . . .

'One April, we left Vietnam by boat and drifted for several days before we arrived at Bei Hai [on the coast of China]. We repaired our boat and stocked up with food and fuel. We arrived in Hong Kong at the end of May. We went into a refugee camp and lived there for one year.

Thousands of Chinese who left Vietnam were put into prison-like camps in Hong Kong.

'I only considered going to the English-speaking countries because I'd learned a bit of English when I was young and I knew English was an international language. In April 1980 we came to Britain to settle.' [4]

5 Chinese people today

Today, as we saw in Chapter 1, Chinese migrant families can be spread all over the world. As more and more generations are born outside China, it is inevitable that they will move countries for all sorts of different reasons. Even a first-generation migrant does not necessarily remain in the same place for the rest of his or her life. He or she may migrate several times. Alternatively, someone may move to one country for only a few years and then return home. Lili Chau, now working in a shop in London's Chinatown, says this:

'I came to Britain three years ago as a student, especially to learn English. It's very difficult to learn English properly in China, you see, and as it's the number one international language I think it's important to be able to speak it well.

'I'll stay here for four more years, because that's the amount of time I think it will take me to become properly fluent. Then I'll return to China where I hope I'll get a really good job. I have no relatives in Britain – they are all in China.'

The Tiananmen Square massacre took place soon after this student protest in Beijing, in May 1989.

These are some other typical life stories:

Mr Phuong was once a fisherman in Vietnam. He escaped to Hong Kong in 1979 and then moved to Canada in 1984. Now living in Toronto, he works as a waiter in a Chinese restaurant.

Mr Tan used to be a street seller in Indonesia but fled from anti-Chinese riots in 1974. He travelled first to Hong Kong and then migrated again to Australia in 1987. Today, he and his family run a take-away food business in Sydney's Chinatown.

Many people – not just Chinese – come to shop in London's Chinese grocery stores.

Wang Dewei (who now calls himself David Wang) left China in 1989 after the demonstrations in Tiananmen Square in Beijing. (These protests, calling for more democracy in China, were brutally put down by the government, killing many people.) Wang went to the USA where he was offered a place to study at the University of California. Once he has finished his course, he hopes to get a job in New York – or maybe London or Singapore.

Today, many migrant Chinese feel more 'rooted', or settled, abroad than they did fifty or sixty years ago. Although they will always have very strong ties to their ancestral home, they do not necessarily want to return there. Nowadays, a Chinese couple living in Hong Kong might actually wish to retire to Vancouver, for example, to have a quieter life.

Hong Kong

Chinese people have been flowing in and out of Hong Kong ever since the island was leased to Britain in 1842. Seven out of ten of its inhabitants have come from mainland China, or have a parent who did. The population is also made up of many people who fled from persecution in other parts of South East Asia.

(Right) Hong Kong has grown massively since the British took it over in 1842. It is now a major world centre for finance and Chinese culture.

Since the 1950s, Hong Kong has been a very successful commercial centre. Many people have become very wealthy there and, on average, Hong Kong Chinese are thirty-five times richer than their relatives in mainland China.

Most of the Chinese videos and magazines in this shop in Sydney will have been made in Hong Kong.

Hong Kong creates fashions for Chinese living abroad. Most Chinese films and videos, for example, are made in Hong Kong and exported to Chinese communities around the world. Chinese newspapers in different capital cities all mention what is happening in Hong Kong (and China) as well as what is going on in their own countries.

However, the British lease on Hong Kong finishes in 1997, and it will be given back to China. Many people believe that it will no longer be a good place in which to live and work. This is why many thousands of Chinese are now migrating from Hong Kong every year. Between 1986 and 1989, for example, 5.7 million Chinese left for Canada, the USA, Australia and Britain.

CHINESE BUSINESS PEOPLE TODAY

Sally Aw is one of Aw Boon Haw's daughters. When he died in 1954, she inherited one of the newspapers that he owned, the *Sing Tao Daily*. It was not long before she had made it the centre of the largest newspaper empire in Hong Kong. The paper now sells editions in San Francisco, New York, London, Sydney, Toronto and Vancouver. Sally Aw has been made an Officer of the British Empire (OBE) and was the first woman to be elected as Chairman of the International Press Institute.

Another well-known Chinese business person is Li Ka-shing, one of the richest men in the world. However, he was not always a billionaire. Born in southern China, he arrived as a refugee in Hong Kong in 1940, at the age of twelve.

Two years later his father died and Li Ka-shing had to leave school and look after his family. He went to work in a factory. Gradually, he became a salesman, a manager and then, at twenty-two, he started his own company. Over the years, this business has turned into an empire that includes supermarkets, property, oil companies and shares in newspaper and book publishing companies world-wide. [5]

Mr Li, a self-made billionaire, has been called 'the man with the golden touch'.

Chinese people in Britain

The Chinese living in Britain come mostly from Hong Kong (though some are from Vietnam, Singapore, Malaysia and China). Chinese men started arriving in large numbers in the 1950s because they could no longer make a living from farming, and because Britain needed more labour during that period. (They migrated because of both 'push' and 'pull' factors.) Then, in the 1960s and 1970s, their wives and children migrated to join them. By 1981, over 25 per cent of the Chinese in Britain had been born in the country and, by 1985, there were an estimated 122,000 in the community.

The Chinese quickly saw opportunities in the catering trade, and today, about 80 per cent of them make a living from businesses such as restaurants, take-away food shops and supermarkets. Whereas in the 1950s there was only a handful of Chinese restaurants in Britain, by the mid-1980s there were about 7,000 of them.

Many Chinese families have members living all over the world.

The family group is still very important to the Chinese living in Britain. The father is the leader of the family and he and his wife do their best to ensure that their children do not lose their customs, beliefs or language. If a family has difficulties, it will call on the support of close relatives and friends first of all before asking for help from non-Chinese people and government officials.

By establishing themselves so strongly in the catering trade in Britain, the Chinese play a part in British society which is appreciated by non-Chinese people. However, life is not always easy for them. For example, about 70 per cent of the first-generation immigrants are unable to speak English. Also, in 1984, it was found that only 52 per cent of Chinese pupils in secondary schools were fluent in English. These language problems cause difficulties in communication, in passing exams and in getting good jobs. Also, because they have to work such long hours in the restaurants and shops, there is not much time or opportunity to get better at English. Sometimes, the British are not especially friendly towards them either.

Kim, a Chinese worker in a take-away food shop in South London explains:

'I came here from Hong Kong three years ago and then my sister joined me shortly afterwards. I work from 5 p.m. to 1 a.m. and so I have the days free.

'I'd like to get to know British people my age but it's not always easy for us to understand each other – and sometimes they don't seem very interested in trying, to be honest. My sister and I don't have any other family here so we do a lot together. We could go into Chinatown in central London but although there are Chinese people there, we don't know any of them either. It's nice here, but sometimes it's a bit lonely.'

Chinese restaurants are found all over the world, in many different countries.

JUNG CHANG AND AMY TAN

Jung Chang is the author of *Wild Swans*, a best-selling book about the lives of her grandmother, her mother and herself in China. Not only is it the unforgettable story of three women, but it also gives a fascinating picture of the enormous changes which have occurred in China during this century.

Jung Chang was born in Sichuan Province in China in 1952. She left the country in 1978 to study English in Britain, and now lives in London.

Jung Chang receiving an award in London for her book Wild Swans.

Amy Tan was born in California, also in 1952, several years after her parents emigrated to the USA. Her first novel, *The Joy Luck Club*, was published in 1989. It is based on stories told by Tan's mother about her life in China, and about the relationship between women born in the USA to Chinese parents, and their mothers. The book has been extremely successful, and has now been made into a film.

Amy Tan says that, like many American-born Chinese, she has had some difficulties in understanding the parts of her that are Chinese, and the parts that are American.

Amy Tan, well-known for her books about Chinese-Americans.

Chinese in the USA, Canada and Australia

In the USA, the story is different. An enormous number of Chinese migrants have entered the country during the last thirty years. For example, by 1985 there were four times more Chinese in the USA than there had been in 1960. There is now about one Chinese person for every hundred people in the USA.

Most of the recent Chinese migrants in the USA come from Taiwan, China, the countries of South East Asia and from Hong Kong. They do not appear to have so many difficulties learning English and this means they can make more use of educational opportunities.

Jenny Kee is a Chinese Australian who is now one of the country's most famous designers. In 1973 she opened a small shop in Sydney, stocking her colourful fabric and knitwear designs which are often inspired by Australia's plants, animals and Aboriginal culture. By the end of the 1970s her clothes were not only selling well in Sydney, but were also beginning to be popular in other parts of Australia too.

Chinese-Canadian children enjoying themselves in Vancouver.

JENNY KEE

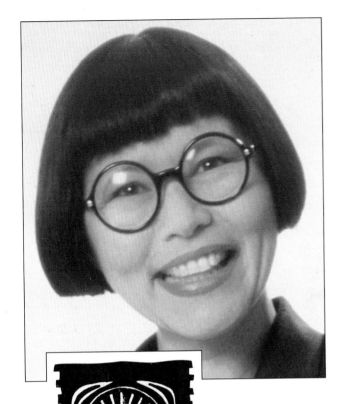

Her international breakthrough came in 1982 when Princess Diana was photographed wearing a Jenny Kee sweater. Then the well-known fashion designer Karl Lagerfeld used her textiles for his clothes. Soon, Kee's designs were being sold in New York, Paris, Milan, London, Los Angeles and Tokyo. [6]

Jenny Kee, who lives and works in Sydney. The city has a large, and growing, Chinese community.

As a result, they find jobs in almost every area of work. Some have become famous, including: Tsung-dao Lee, winner of the Nobel Prize; Yo-yo Ma, the well-known cellist; I M Pei, the architect who designed the glass pyramid in front of the Louvre in Paris; and Betty Bao Lord, the novelist.

In some Canadian cities the presence of Chinese people is much more noticeable than in US cities. That is because nearly all the 600,000 Chinese in Canada live in Toronto and Vancouver. Although in Canada as a whole two out of every hundred people are Chinese, in Vancouver, one out of every five people is of Chinese background.

6 Chinese culture

A concentration of Chinese shops, offices and places to live is usually called 'Chinatown'. Most of the large cities of the world, such as London, New York, San Francisco, Paris, Toronto, Vancouver, Bangkok, Yokohama and Sydney, have their own Chinatown.

New York's Chinatown started in 1844. Although it was estimated that by 1988 there were 300,000 ethnic Chinese living in the city, not all of them lived in Chinatown. However, it is an area where they can meet each other, and go for entertainment, shopping and business.

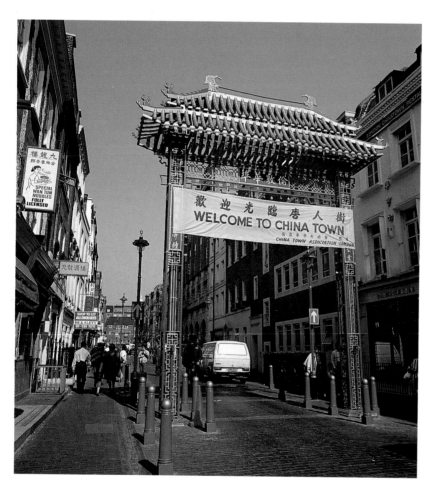

The ornamental gate to London's Chinatown.

Britain's largest Chinatown is in London and is comparatively recent. It started to grow in 1965, when five Chinese restaurants opened in Gerrard Street. Soon, other Chinese businesses moved to join them.

Today, many nearby streets in the district of Soho are humming with Chinese life. Here, you can buy Chinese groceries, eat in Chinese restaurants, and buy books and newspapers written in Chinese languages. If you are having legal difficulties, you can go to the Chinese Community Centre in Gerrard Street and ask advice from an expert. At this centre, you can also leave your young children in the playgroup or take classes in English. On Sunday mornings, you can go there just to meet and talk to other Chinese people.

Whether you are Chinese or not, Chinatowns are good places to get an idea of modern life in the local Chinese community. You can learn a lot just by wandering around, going into the shops, trying some of the special Chinese foods being sold, listening to Chinese music and so on. Chinatowns are also the places where festivals are held. The Chinese New Year, for example, is celebrated in London's Chinatown with a colourful procession. Firecrackers are let off, the streets are decorated, and many Chinese and other people come to the area to enjoy themselves.

Chinese New Year celebrations in Chinatown, Washington D.C. People of all nationalities come to enjoy the colourful festival.

Another interesting place worth visiting is a Chinese herbalist, or chemist's shop. Chinese medicine has been practised for thousands of years in China and can be divided into two parts: acupuncture (inserting very fine needles into the body) and herbal therapy (the drinking of specific herbal teas). The aim is to put the body back in balance again and make the patient feel well.

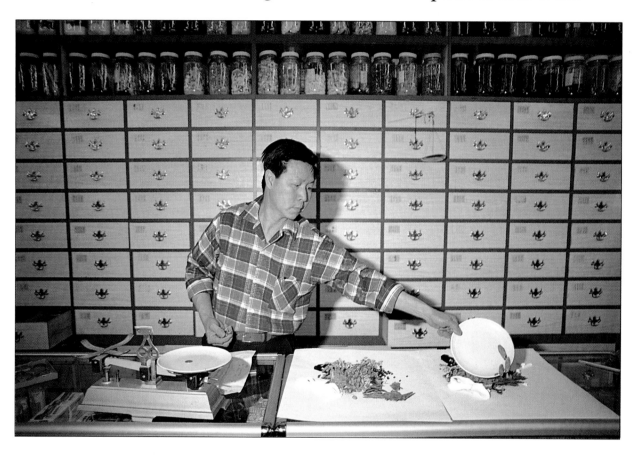

A herbalist's shop in the suburbs of Sydney. The herbs are stored in the drawers and jars and are measured out when needed.

When someone who is feeling ill has visited a Chinese doctor, he or she takes the prescription to the herbalist. Inside the shop there is usually a wall of small wooden drawers, as well as many glass bottles and other containers. These are full of the different herbs which the patient will add to water and drink as a tea. The herbs are collected and dried in mainland China and come from flowers, plants, the bark of trees, leaves and other similar sources. The herbalist weighs out the correct amount of these dried plants, according to the prescription.

Chinese medicine is known to be particularly good for treating skin problems. In London, for example, the surgery of a herbalist practising in Chinatown is visited by both Chinese and non-Chinese people, and there are always long queues of patients waiting to see her. She has become so well known for treating eczema that Western skin specialists in a nearby hospital would like to learn the secrets of her success.

As you walk around Chinatown, you will also see many Chinese restaurants. Food and cooking are of great importance to the Chinese so it is natural that some migrants will become involved in the catering trade in their new countries.

HOW TO USE CHOPSTICKS

Chopsticks were invented at least 3,000 years ago in China. The Chinese use them instead of knives and forks, but it takes quite a lot of practice before you can pick up food easily with them.

I Hold one between your thumb, first and second fingers, like a pencil. This chopstick is supposed to move like a lever.

2 Take the other chopstick and place one end into the angle of your hand, between your thumb and first finger. Slide its other end between the ends of your third and fourth fingers. This chopstick is held steady. When used correctly, the chopsticks act as a kind of pincer.

Don't be surprised if it takes a little time to get used to chopsticks. You will be an expert when you can pick up three peanuts at once!

China is a huge country and different regions have different styles of cooking. For example, in the north (which includes Beijing), dishes contain a lot of ginger and garlic and the food is relatively heavy. In the east (around the Yangtse delta) people eat a lot of fish and enjoy sweet dishes. Food from the west of China (including Sichuan) is likely to seem hot and is spiced with pepper and chillies. The cooking in the south, however, contains a great deal of fish and also includes many small snacks called *dimsum*. This southern food includes that from Canton. There is a Chinese joke about food which says that the people in Canton 'eat everything with wings except aeroplanes and everything with legs except the table'!

Dimsum *come in many shapes, sizes and delicious flavours. They include dumplings made with meat or fish, steamed buns, small crunchy rolls and pieces of spicy meat.*

The kind of cooking which is offered in Chinese restaurants depends on which part of China the chef has come from. This principle also applies to other things you might see as you finish your walk round Chinatown. Notice the different faces that people have – these may indicate whether they come originally from, say, the north or the south of China. Notice, too, all the different kinds of books and papers in the newsagents as well as all the unusual sorts of food in the Chinese supermarkets. Try to find out if there is a temple nearby, and ask if you can look inside to see what is happening.

BIRD'S NEST SOUP

The Chinese consider bird's nest a great delicacy. Any old bird's nest will not do – it has to be the nest of a particular kind of small swift. It collects moss and feathers and other bits and pieces and sticks them (in the shape of nests) to the roof of caves with its saliva.

It is not surprising that by the time they reach shops around the world the nests are very expensive. In London, for example, a 100g box of bird's nest from North Borneo costs £38.

The nests are believed to give better health, particularly to men. They can be served in many different kinds of sweet or savoury soups.

All these things will show you how much history and culture the Chinese person brings when coming to live in another country. If he or she is a first-generation migrant there will have been influence from either push or pull factors before leaving – and he or she may have lived in several different countries already. If a second or third-generation Chinese, he or she may feel fully or only partly attached to the new country. However, whatever the circumstances, the Chinese migrant helps to enrich the new country by sharing parts of the fascinating Chinese way of life.

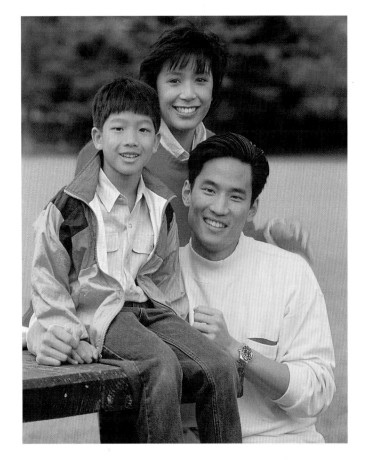

Many Chinese people become well integrated into their new countries.

Glossary

Acupuncture The treatment of diseases by inserting very thin needles through the skin at carefully chosen places.

Addictive A way of describing a drug that affects people so much they depend on it.

Ancestor A person from whom you are directly descended, usually further back than a grandparent.

Bound feet A fashion in China to limit the size of women's feet, as it was believed that very small feet were attractive. When she was about seven years old, a girl's feet were bound up so that the toes were bent under the sole of the foot. The process was extremely painful.

Communism A system of organizing people where land or housing is owned by a community rather than single people, and each person works for the benefit of all.

Democracy A form of government where all the people have a say in what is decided, either directly, or by choosing a representative.

Discrimination Treating certain group of people badly because of negative feelings about their skin colour, language, religion, culture or political beliefs.

Emigrate To leave one country in order to settle in another.

Empire A collection of peoples, territories and countries under the rule of one person or government.

Ethnic Chinese A description meaning that all Chinese people – even though they live in different countries or speak different languages – come from the same Chinese race.

Family tree A chart showing the relationships and different generations of one family.

Generation A group of people born at roughly the same time. For example, all the children in a family are in one generation. Their parents and their parents' brothers and sisters are in another generation.

Homeland The country in which a person was born.

Indentured labour Work agreed between a worker and a master, and sealed by a written contract.

Indigenous Coming from, or naturally occurring in, a country or region.

Inscrutable Impossible to understand, or very mysterious.

Khmer Rouge The Kampuchean Communist Party. Its brutal policies caused the deaths of thousands of people in Cambodia, especially the ethnic Chinese.

Lodging houses Places offering a temporary place to sleep and, sometimes, meals as well.

Looting Stealing from places that are unprotected after violent events, such as riots or war.

Lease An agreement where one person (or government) allows another to occupy land for a set period of time.

Mutiny Rebellion against authority, usually by soldiers, or on board a ship.

Opium A drug made from the opium poppy.

Population explosion A rapid increase in the number of people living in a country or city.

Prejudice An opinion against, or in favour of, a person or thing, often made in ignorance. It is possible to have a prejudice against foreigners, or people of another race.

Race A general word for a group of people who share the same ancestors, and may look similar. They may have the same type of hair, colour of eyes and skin, and other physical characteristics.

Racist Belief that people's abilities and characteristics are influenced by what race they belong to.

Refugee Someone who has fled from danger, often from one country to another.

Remittance Money sent regularly, often through the post.

Stereotype An idea or belief that is often repeated, and no longer has much truth in it.

Tribute Money paid by one country or ruler to another, to pay for peace or for trading rights. a present, as a mark of respect.

Find out more

Books to read

Ancient China by Robert Nicholson and Claire Watts (Franklin Watts, London, 1991)
The Ancient Chinese (Heinemann Children's Reference, Oxford, 1992)
China, by Julia Waterlow (Wayland, Hove, UK, 1993)
China Since 1945 by Stewart Ross (Wayland, Hove, UK, 1988)
Chinese Americans by William Dayley (Chelsea House, USA, 1987)
Exploring Chinese Food in Britain by Jessie Lim (Mantra Publishing, UK, 1989)
Food Around the World: Taste of China by Roz Denny (Wayland, Hove, UK, 1994)

Further information for teachers

Films:

Dim Sum, directed by Wayne Wang, is a modest but very appealing film about a Westernized Chinese family in San Francisco. (1985, available on video.)

Man from China is a short feature by Zhang Tielin, a former movie star in China, now an exile in Britain. It deals with the experiences of a young Chinese painter who comes to London soon after the Beijing massacre, and his difficulties in adjusting to a different society (1990).

The Joy Luck Club is adapted from Amy Tan's novel of the same name, and is about US-born women from Chinese families, and their relationships with their mothers (1994).

Books about Chinese people:

Amy Tan's novels, *The Joy Luck Club* (Minerva, London, 1992) and *The Kitchen God's Wife* (Collins, London, 1993) deal with the experiences of Chinese-American women and their Chinese-born mothers.

Sour Sweet by Timothy Mo, (Vintage, London, 1992). A novel about a Chinese family in Britain who run a take-away food shop in London's East End, while hiding from the city's Chinese gangsters.

Wild Swans: Three Daughters of China by Jung Chang (Flamingo, London, 1993). An extraordinary account of the lives of three women living in China: the author's grandmother (born in 1909) her mother and herself, up until she left China in 1978.

Other sources of information include:

The Needs of the Chinese Community in the North West published by the Commission for Racial Equality (Elliot House, Allington Street, London SW1, Tel 071 828 7022) 1987.

The Chinese, Portrait of a People by John Fraser (Collins, London, 1980).

The Chinese Community in Britain, 1984–5 Second Committee Report from the Home Affairs Committee: HMSO, London, 1985.

A Companion to China by Frances Wood (Weidenfeld & Nicolson, London, 1988).

The Chinese of South-East Asia, Minority Rights Group (379 Brixton Road, London SW9 7DE, Tel 071 978 9498) 1992.

Notes on sources

1 *Sons of the Yellow Emperor: Story of the Overseas Chinese* by Lynn Pan (Mandarin, London, 1991)
2 *Sons of the Yellow Emperor*, as above
3 *The Spectator*, London, 30 June, 1979
4 *Hackney Pensioners' Press*, London, date unknown.
5 *Sons of the Yellow Emperor*, as above
6 *Made for Australia* by Judith Kendra (Harcourt Brace Jovanovich, Australia, 1990)

Index

Entries in **bold** indicate subjects shown in pictures as well as in the text.

PICTURE ACKNOWLEDGEMENTS
Archiv fur Kunst und Geschichte, Berlin 11, 12, 14; Associated Press 25, 27; The Bettman Archive 19; Camera Press 7 (Joachim Messerschmidt), 11 top (F Fischbeck), 21 top (F Fischbeck), 28 (Chris Davies), 29 (Chris Davies), 40 (Nicholas Holt), 44 (F Fischbeck); Chapel Studios 38; Eye Ubiquitous 6, 8 (Julia Waterlow), 10 (Simon Arnold), 26 (Tim Page), 32 (Matthew McKee), 33 (P Thompson), 42 (Matthew McKee); Impact 31 (John Cole); Peter Newark's Historical Pictures 13, 15, 17 (bottom), 18, 20 (bottom), 23, 24; Photri Inc 41 (Lisa Sardan; Rex Features (Sipa Press) 30-31; Robert Harding imprint and contents page (Adam Woolfitt), 9 (Adam Woolfitt), 17 (top), 36 (Adam Woolfitt), 45; Royal Commonwealth Society Collection 22; Topham Picture Source 20 (top), 34, 35, 37 (John Stillwell); Wayland (Z Mukhida) cover and title page.